PRAYERS FOR MY FUTURE HUSBAND

The Ultimate 31 Prayer Guide To Preparing Your Heart For Him

Evangelist James Roland

Music Playlist

TABLE OF CONTENTS

Inside Paperback Of this Book you Will have access to 20 free journal prayer

INTRODUCTION

Welcome to this collection of heartfelt prayers—each one crafted with love, hope, and faith for the man who will one day be your husband. Within these pages, you'll find a tapestry of prayers intended to uplift, support, and guide your future partner as he journeys through life, awaiting the moment your paths will intertwine.

The decision to compile these prayers emerged from a deep desire to express care not only for the man you have yet to meet but also for the relationship you hope to nurture and build with him. Each prayer is a whisper to the divine, a heartfelt plea for blessings, guidance, and grace upon the life of your future husband.

As a pastor, I have witnessed the power of prayer in transforming lives, guiding decisions, and fostering spiritual growth. These prayers are not just mere words; they are an offering of faith and an expression of devotion to the man who will one day share your life's journey.

Throughout these pages, you'll discover prayers that touch upon various facets of your future husband's life—his spiritual growth, emotional well-being, relationships, career, health, and his role within the community. Each prayer is carefully composed to reflect the aspirations you hold for him, echoing the sentiments of love, support, and encouragement that you wish to extend.

The beauty of prayer lies not only in its ability to invoke divine blessings but also in its capacity to transform the heart of the one who prays. As you delve into these prayers, may you find solace, strength, and a deepened connection with the divine, knowing that your intentions are heard and embraced by the universe.

I encourage you to personalize these prayers, infusing them with your own hopes, dreams, and aspirations for your future husband. Feel free to adapt, modify, or elaborate on these words to resonate more closely with your heart's desires.

May these prayers serve as a guiding light, a source of comfort, and a reminder of the love that awaits both you and your future husband. May they pave the way for a relationship grounded in faith, love, and mutual respect, flourishing under the grace of the divine.

May your journey through these prayers be one of anticipation, hope, and unwavering belief in the beautiful future that lies ahead.

PREPARATION AND
SPIRITUAL GROWTH

We explore prayers in this section that focus on your prospective husband's spiritual path. These prayers are meant to boost the man's spirit, encourage a closer relationship with God, and prepare the path for his spiritual development as you wait for him to show up.

A life together requires more than just hoping to meet someone amazing; it also includes being mentally, emotionally, and spiritually ready. Your dedication to helping your future spouse have a closer relationship with God is demonstrated by these prayers.

A Prayer for His Relationship with God

Heavenly Father,

I come before you today with a prayer for my future husband, the man you will someday bring into my life. Though I haven't yet met him, my heart desires your perfect will for him, especially in his relationship with you. Lord, I pray that he would know you deeply and personally. May he experience your love, grace, and forgiveness in a way that transforms him from the inside out. Lead him to your Word, grant him wisdom to understand its truths, and fill him with the Holy Spirit's guidance to follow your ways. Grant him a growing hunger for righteousness and a heart sensitive to your voice. Equip him with the strength to resist temptation and the courage to stand firm in his faith, even in times of challenge. Make him a man of prayer, one who finds comfort and direction in your presence. Shape him into a servant leader, someone who seeks to honor you in all he does and who uses his gifts and talents to bless others. Guide him to a community of believers who will encourage and support him in his walk with you. Father, I trust your timing and understand that you will bring him into my life at the perfect moment. In the meantime, I pray that you would prepare both of us for the day we meet. Help me to grow in my own faith and become the woman you desire me to be for him.

May our future marriage be rooted in Christ, built on a foundation of love, respect, and shared values. May we be partners in serving you and fulfilling your purpose for our lives together.

Thank you, Lord, for the incredible gift of love and the promise of a future family. I surrender my desires to your will and trust you to guide me every step of the way.

In your holy name, I pray. Amen.

Proverbs 3:5-6 (NIV)
Trust in the Lord with all your heart and lean not on your own understanding; in all your ways submit to him, and he will make your paths straight.

Prayer for Wisdom and Discernment

Heavenly Father,

Grant my future husband wisdom and discernment in all his decisions. Help him rely on Your wisdom and guidance in every aspect of his life.

IN JESUS NAME I PRAY AMEN

Jeremiah 29:11 (NIV)

For I know the plans I have for you," declares the Lord, "plans to prosper you and not to harm you, plans to give you hope and a future

Prayer for Strength in Challenges

Heavenly Father

Lord, in times of adversity, may my future husband find his strength in You. Grant him courage and resilience to face challenges, knowing that You are his refuge.

In Jesus Name I Pray Amen

Psalm 32:8 (NIV)

I will instruct you and teach you in the way you should go; I will counsel you with my loving eye on you.

Prayer for Spiritual Protection

Heavenly Father,

I come before you today filled with anticipation and hope for the future, particularly for the man who will one day become my husband. Though I wait on your perfect timing for our paths to cross, I already lift him up in prayer, asking for your continual protection and guidance.

Shield him, Lord, from spiritual darkness. Guard his heart and mind from negativity, doubt, and any influence that would lead him astray from your light. Fill him with your discernment and grace to identify and resist spiritual temptations.

Empower him with a warrior's spirit. Equip him with the armor of your truth, righteousness, and faith. Grant him courage to stand for what is right, even when the world may challenge him. Let his voice be strong in defending your name and spreading love.

Guide his steps towards you. Surround him with your divine presence, leading him closer to your wisdom and grace. Open his eyes to your goodness and the beauty of your creation. May he yearn for a deeper relationship with you.

Bless him with a heart overflowing with compassion. Instill

in him a generous spirit, always ready to love, forgive, and serve others. Grant him the gift of empathy and understanding, allowing him to be a source of comfort and strength for those around him.

Father, I trust your perfect plan for me and my future husband. When the time comes, guide our paths to converge, and may our love be a reflection of your divine love in the world. Until then, I entrust him to your care, confident that you will watch over him, protect him, and prepare him for the blessings we will one day share.

In your holy name, I pray, Amen.

EMOTIONAL WELL-BEING AND INNER PEACE

This section includes prayers aimed at fostering your future husband's emotional health.

These prayers are meant to surround the guy who is meant to be your partner in life's pleasures and difficulties with emotional fortitude, serenity, and satisfaction.

One of the main components of a successful and resilient existence is emotional well-being. These prayers are designed to help your future spouse navigate his emotional journey by offering comfort in trying moments and cultivating inner calm that is independent of external events.

Prayer for Inner Peace

Dear Divine Source,

I pray for my future husband, the guy I will one day share my life and journey with, as I come before you today. I cherish him in my heart and spirit, even if I haven't seen him in person. I pray for his ultimate well-being, especially for inner peace.

Give him a calm assurance that comes from within, O Source, unaffected by circumstances or outside approval. May he realize that, rooted in your grace and purpose, he is deserving of love and acceptance.

Help him discover constructive ways to achieve inner calm, whether it's via contemplation, meditation, a hug from nature, or the comfort of company. Allow him to learn techniques that will nourish his spirit and give him the fortitude to overcome the inevitable obstacles in life.

Give him steadfast trust in your omnipresence, a source of strength that flows through uncertainty and gloom. May he take solace in the understanding that your love is always there for him and that he is never alone.

Bless him with an observant heart and a kind disposition, able to also bring serenity to others. Wherever he goes, may he be a lighthouse of peace and compassion, sharing your love and encouraging sincere communication.

In the end, my Divine Source, I ask that you guide him toward me at the appropriate moment, when our paths are both clear of inner turmoil and prepared to merge. May our love serve as a safe haven where harmony prevails for one another.

I'm grateful that you heard my prayer and that you will continue to lead me on this amazing life adventure. I have faith in your omniscience and impeccable timing.

AMEN

Prayer for Healing

"Dear Heavenly Father,

I come before you with a heart full of hope and faith, lifting up my future husband to your loving care. I pray for his healing, both physically and emotionally. May your divine presence surround him, bringing comfort, strength, and restoration to every part of his being.

Lord, I ask for your healing touch to mend any wounds, ailments, or illnesses he may be facing. Grant him the resilience to overcome any health challenges and bless him with vitality and wholeness. May your healing power flow through his body, renewing him in mind, body, and spirit.

Father, I also pray for emotional healing. If there are any past hurts, anxieties, or burdens weighing on his heart, I ask that you bring peace and healing. Grant him the courage to release any pain and grant him a heart filled with joy and tranquility.

Lord, prepare and strengthen both of us for the beautiful journey ahead. Help us grow individually in our relationship with you so that together, we may build a strong, loving, and supportive union based on faith, trust, and mutual respect.
I commit my future husband into your loving hands, trusting in your perfect timing and plan for our lives. May your grace and blessings be upon him today and always.

In Jesus' name, I pray, Amen."

Psalm 34:17-18 (NIV)

The righteous cry out, and the Lord hears them; he delivers them from all their troubles. The Lord is close to the brokenhearted and saves those who are crushed in spirit.

Prayer for Joy and Happiness

Dear heavenly Father

Lord, fill my future husband's life with moments of joy, laughter, and genuine happiness. Help him see the beauty in everyday blessings.

AMEN

JOHN 14:27 (NIV)

Peace I leave with you; my peace I give you. I do not give to you as the world gives. Do not let your hearts be troubled and do not be afraid.

Prayer for Emotional Resilience

Dear Lord,

As I contemplate the possibility of marriage and the man who might one day share my life, I lift up a prayer for his emotional well-being, particularly for his strength and resilience in the face of challenges.

Grant him, O Lord, a heart fortified by your love and grace. May he find his anchor in you, especially during periods of darkness and doubt. Let his faith be a shield against the storms of life, helping him navigate hardships with courage and composure.

Bless him with an innate resilience, the ability to bounce back from setbacks and disappointments. Equip him with the emotional tools to process difficult emotions healthily, finding solace and wisdom in introspection and self-reflection. Give him the strength to seek support when needed, knowing that vulnerability is not weakness but a sign of courage and self-awareness.

Guide him, Lord, in developing healthy coping mechanisms. May he find solace in activities that nurture his spirit and replenish his emotional reserves. Grant him wisdom in discerning healthy boundaries and maintaining a balanced well-being.

Fill him with empathy and compassion, not only for himself but for others around him. Give him the ability to listen with an open heart and understand the emotions of others without taking them on as his own.

May he be a source of strength and comfort for those he loves, offering support and understanding during their own times of struggle.

Lord, I pray that if he is the one destined to be my partner, we may create a safe haven for each other, a space where both vulnerability and resilience are celebrated. May we support each other in navigating life's joys and sorrows, building a bond strengthened by faith, compassion, and unwavering love.

IN YOUR HOLY NAME, I PRAY. AMEN.

NURTURING RELATIONSHIPS

This section contains prayers intended to help your future husband develop meaningful relationships. These prayers are intended to bless the man's relationships with family, friends, and most importantly, the one that will ultimately unite your hearts, as you eagerly await his union with the one who is meant to accompany you on your journey.

Our lives are woven together by the relationships we have, which provide us with love, compassion, and support. The purpose of these prayers is to bless the relationships that mold and enhance the life of your future spouse.

Prayer for Family Harmony

"DEAR LORD,

I come before you with a grateful heart, thanking you for the gift of love and the promise of a future partner. I pray for my future husband, wherever he may be, that you guide him and protect him in all his endeavors.

God, bless the relationships my future husband has with his family. May there be love, understanding, and unity among them.

AMEN

Proverbs 17:17 (NIV)

A friend loves at all times, and a brother is born for a time of adversity.

Prayer for Friendships

Heavenly Father,

I entrust the future of my husband's friendships to your care. Guide him in cultivating and cherishing relationships that will enrich his life and draw him closer to you. Bless him with friends who share his values and aspirations. May they inspire him to grow spiritually, intellectually, and emotionally. Let them be a source of encouragement and support in times of trouble, and let them celebrate his victories with heartfelt joy.

Grant him friendships that are built on mutual respect and trust. May these bonds be filled with open communication, genuine empathy, and unwavering loyalty. Guide him to be a friend who is dependable, understanding, and always ready to lend a listening ear.

Fill his life with diverse friendships that broaden his horizons. Grant him companions who offer new perspectives, challenge his assumptions, and introduce him to different cultures and experiences. May these connections foster humility, understanding, and a deeper appreciation for the world around him.

Lead him to friendships that are grounded in your love. May his relationships reflect your values of forgiveness, kindness, and selflessness. Guide him to be a friend who brings your light into the lives of others.

Protect him from harmful friendships that could lead him astray. Grant him discernment to recognize negative influences and the strength to walk away from relationships that do not serve him or your purpose for his life.

Lord, I know that you desire for your children to find love and support in strong, healthy friendships. Please guide my future husband in fostering these connections. May his life be enriched by the joy, encouragement, and wisdom he finds in his companions, and may his friendships ultimately draw him closer to you.

In your name I pray, Amen.

Prayer for Our Future Relationship

Dearest God,

I come before you today with a heart filled with hope and anticipation for the future husband and the loving relationship we will build together. I trust in your perfect timing and know that you will bring him into my life when it is the right moment.

For him, I pray for a man of strong character and unwavering faith. May he be guided by your love and walk in your light. Grant him a kind and compassionate heart, capable of understanding and supporting me through life's joys and challenges. Bless him with wisdom and intelligence, but also with a playful spirit and an adventurous soul.

I pray that our future relationship will be a vibrant tapestry woven with trust, respect, and open communication. May we cherish each other's strengths and accept each other's flaws, knowing that together we can overcome any obstacle. Fill our love with laughter and passion, but also with gentle moments of shared comfort and understanding.

Guide me, Lord, to become the woman he needs me to be. Help me cultivate patience, empathy, and unconditional love. Grant me the strength to support his dreams and the wisdom to be a true partner in his journey. Ultimately, I entrust our future relationship to your hands. Guide our paths, lead us to one another, and bless our union with your enduring love. I pray that together, we may build a home filled with your grace and a life that glorifies your name.

In Jesus Name I pray Amen.

Prayer for Patience and Understanding

"Heavenly Father,

I come to you with a heart full of hope and love, lifting up my future husband before you. I pray for an outpouring of patience and understanding upon him.

Grant him the patience to navigate life's challenges, to wait upon Your timing, and to trust in Your plans for his life. May he find solace in moments of uncertainty and strength in times of trial, knowing that Your wisdom surpasses all understanding.

Grant him a deep sense of understanding, Lord. Help him to comprehend the complexities of life, relationships, and the needs of others. May he have the empathy to listen and the wisdom to discern, fostering connections built on understanding and compassion.

Prepare his heart and mind, Lord, to embrace the beauty of patience and understanding in all aspects of life, especially in our future relationship. May our bond be strengthened by these virtues, creating a foundation of love, respect, and harmony.

I entrust his journey into Your loving hands, knowing that You have a perfect plan for him. Guide him, mold him, and equip him with the virtues necessary to be a wonderful partner.

IN JESUS' NAME, I PRAY.

AMEN."

CAREER, ENDEAVORS, AND FINANCIAL STABILITY

This section is devoted to prayers regarding your prospective husband's career and financial situation. These prayers ask for blessings for the man who is meant to accompany you on your journey, as well as for his work, endeavors, and steadiness in handling money.

Both a successful career and sound financial standing are essential elements of a happy existence. The purpose of these prayers is to ask God to direct and provide benefits for your future husband's career and financial security.

Prayer for Career Direction

Heavenly Father,

I lift up my future husband before you today, praying for your guiding hand in his career direction. Grant him clarity and wisdom as he navigates his path, revealing his unique talents and passions.

Lord, you know his heart's desires, the dreams he holds close. Open doors that align with his skills and purpose, leading him to work that will not only provide for him, but also bring him fulfillment and satisfaction.

Guide his decision-making, granting him discernment to identify opportunities that offer challenge, growth, and a chance to make a positive impact. Protect him from paths that may lure him with empty promises but lack true meaning.

Bless him with resilience in the face of obstacles, confidence in his abilities, and courage to step outside his comfort zone. Surround him with mentors and colleagues who encourage him, inspire him, and share his values.

May his work be a source of blessing not only for him, but also for those around him. Grant him the wisdom to use his talents and resources to benefit others, making a positive contribution to the world.

Above all, Lord, fill him with your peace and guidance. Let him know that he is not alone in this journey, but that you are walking beside him every step of the way.

In your holy name, I pray. Amen.

Prayer for Success

"Dear Heavenly Father,

I come before you today with a heart full of hope and gratitude. I lift up my future husband to You, asking for Your divine guidance and blessings upon his life.

Please grant him the strength and determination to pursue his dreams and endeavors. May success, in all its forms, manifest abundantly in his life. Bless him with wisdom, resilience, and perseverance in the face of challenges. Grant him favor in his work, relationships, and every area of his life. May he find fulfillment and joy in his endeavors and experience the fruit of his hard work. Help him to make wise decisions that align with Your will and purpose for his life.

Lord, surround him with mentors, friends, and opportunities that will encourage and uplift him on his journey to success. May he be a beacon of light and positivity in the world, using his achievements to make a positive impact on others.

I pray for protection over him, guarding his heart, mind, and spirit against negativity and discouragement. May Your love and grace be his constant companion.

Prepare me, Lord, to be a supportive and loving partner to him, celebrating his successes and walking with him through the challenges. Help me to be a source of strength and encouragement in his life.

Thank you, Lord, for hearing this prayer. May Your blessings flow abundantly upon my future husband, guiding him toward a future filled with success, happiness, and fulfillment.

In Jesus' name, Amen."

Prayer for Financial Stability

"Dear Heavenly Father,

I come to You with a prayer for my future husband's financial stability. I pray that You will bless him with wisdom, discernment, and the ability to make sound financial decisions. Please grant him the strength to persevere through any financial challenges he may face and the wisdom to manage resources wisely.

May he find fulfillment and success in his work or endeavors, and may his efforts be fruitful. Provide him with opportunities for growth and advancement in his career or business pursuits. Grant him the favor of wise counsel and guidance in financial matters.

Help him to be a good steward of his finances, to be responsible with his resources, and to honor You with his financial decisions. May he experience Your abundance and blessings in every aspect of his life.

I pray for Your provision over his life, that he may be blessed with financial stability and security, enabling him to support himself, his loved ones, and contribute positively to the needs of others.

Please grant him peace of mind concerning his finances, knowing that You are his provider and that You will always take care of him. Strengthen our future relationship so that together we may support and encourage each other in times of need.

In Jesus' name, I pray. Amen."

HEALTH AND WELL-BEING

This section is devoted to prayers for your future husband's physical, mental, and emotional well-being. These prayers ask for blessings for the man who is meant to walk alongside you on life's journey, as you eagerly await their union. May he lead a healthy, balanced life.

Being well is a priceless gift that gives us the energy and strength to face life's obstacles. These prayers are designed to ask God for his grace and blessings in order to support your future husband's physical, mental, and emotional well-being.

Prayer for Rest and Renewal

Dearest Heavenly Father,

I entrust my future husband to your loving care, even though I haven't yet met him. I pray for him to find rest and renewal in your presence, for he will face challenges and need your strength to overcome them.

Grant him, Lord, deep and peaceful sleep, where his mind and body can truly restore.

May he wake each morning refreshed and ready to face the day with your light in his eyes.

Fill him with your renewing spirit, washing away any burdens or anxieties that may weigh him down. May he find solace in your word and seek your guidance in times of difficulty.

Let him discover joy in the simple things, in the beauty of nature, the laughter of loved ones, and the quiet moments of solitude with you. Remind him to celebrate even the small victories, for progress is paved with tiny steps.

Bless him with a network of supportive friends and family who can uplift him when he stumbles and encourage him on his journey. May he also be a source of strength and comfort for others, sharing your love with the world.

Finally, Father, I pray for you to guide our paths and reveal your plan for our future. When the time is right, bring us together in your perfect timing, ready to embark on this blessed journey of marriage, forever united in your love.

AMEN.

Prayer for Mental Clarity

Heavenly Father,

As I open my heart to the possibility of love and marriage, I guide my thoughts towards a man blessed with clarity of mind. Grant him, I pray, the strength to navigate life's challenges with a balanced and discerning spirit. May he possess the wisdom to seek understanding and knowledge, the courage to face his vulnerabilities, and the resilience to overcome any mental hurdles that may arise.

May my future husband be blessed with an empathetic heart and a keen awareness of the emotions of others. Guide him to express his own feelings openly and honestly, fostering a relationship built on trust and mutual understanding. Let his clarity extend to the realm of emotional intelligence, allowing him to navigate the complexities of love and connection with wisdom and grace.

Fill my future husband with an insatiable thirst for knowledge and a continuous pursuit of personal growth. Let him embrace intellectual challenges with fervor, finding joy in learning and expanding his horizons. May he be a man who values open communication, critical thinking, and engaging in meaningful conversations that stimulate both his mind and his soul.

Lord, I pray that when our paths converge, we may embark on a journey of mutual understanding and shared support. May his clarity inspire me to seek my own intellectual and emotional growth, and may my strength offer him a safe haven during moments of internal strife. Let our minds resonate with a shared purpose, building a foundation of love and respect that grows ever stronger with time. In faith and with open arms, I surrender this prayer to your divine guidance.

In Jesus Name I Pray Amen.

Prayer for Habits and Self-care

"Dear God,

I come to you today with a heart full of gratitude and hope. I pray for my future husband, whom You know intimately and deeply. As he journeys through life, I ask for Your guidance and grace to cultivate healthy habits and embrace self-care.

Grant him the wisdom to prioritize his well-being, both physically and mentally. Help him to develop habits that nourish his body, mind, and spirit. May he find joy in taking care of himself, understanding that by doing so, he can better serve You and others.

Lord, instill in him the discipline to maintain a balanced lifestyle, to rest when needed, and to make choices that promote his overall health. Grant him the strength to overcome any unhealthy patterns or addictions that may hinder his well-being.

Bless him with resilience and determination to persevere through challenges. May he find solace and rejuvenation in moments of prayer, meditation, and reflection.

Father, may he be surrounded by positive influences and supportive individuals who encourage and uplift him on his journey toward self-improvement.

Above all, I pray that his relationship with You grows stronger each day, for it is in You that he will find ultimate peace, purpose, and fulfillment.

Thank you, Lord, for hearing my prayer. I trust that You will guide and bless my future husband as he navigates his path towards a healthy and fulfilling life.

IN JESUS' NAME, I PRAY, AMEN."

FAITH COMMUNITY AND SERVICE

These prayers focus on your prospective husband's service to others, his involvement in the church community, and his ongoing spiritual development. These prayers ask for blessings for the man who is meant to be your partner's spiritual leader and community involvement as you excitedly await their union.

Two foundational elements that enhance a person's spiritual journey are a thriving faith community and a heart committed to service. The purpose of these prayers is to ask God to guide and bless your future husband in his involvement in a faith community, his service to others, and his spiritual growth.

Prayer for Service and Generosity

"Heavenly Father,

I come to you with a heart full of gratitude for the gift of love and the promise of a future partner.

I lift up my future husband to you, asking for your blessings upon his life.

I pray that you nurture within him a spirit of unwavering service and boundless generosity. May his heart be open to the needs of others, and may he find joy in giving of himself to those around him. Grant him the wisdom to recognize opportunities to serve and the courage to act upon them, selflessly and wholeheartedly.

Instill in him a deep understanding of the power of generosity, not only in material things but in kindness, compassion, and time. Help him to be a beacon of light in the lives of those who cross his path, spreading your love through his actions and words.

Guide him in using his talents and resources to uplift those in need, to be a source of support and encouragement to those who are struggling, and to be a pillar of strength in our community.

Prepare both his heart and mine for a relationship built on mutual respect, understanding, and a shared commitment to serving others. Help us to complement each other in our strengths and weaknesses, supporting one another in our individual journeys toward becoming the best versions of ourselves.

Lord, I trust in your perfect timing and plan for our lives.
May our union be grounded in faith, love, and a shared
desire to make a positive difference in this world.

IN JESUS' NAME, I PRAY,
AMEN."

Prayer for Spiritual Leadership

"Heavenly Father,

I come before you today with a heart full of gratitude for
the gift of love and companionship. I lift up my future
husband to You, asking for Your divine guidance and
blessings upon his life, especially in his role as a spiritual
leader.

Grant him wisdom, Lord, to seek Your will in all things
and to lead our future family with strength and grace. May
he have a heart that seeks after You diligently, finding
solace and strength in Your word. I pray that You deepen
his faith and fill him with Your Holy Spirit so that he may
walk closely with You every day.

Equip him with discernment, patience, and a compassionate spirit as he navigates life's challenges. Help him to exemplify Your love and teachings in all his actions, showing kindness, understanding, and forgiveness to those around him.

Lord, I ask that You prepare both of us for the union that You have planned. Help us to grow individually in our relationship with You so that together, we may glorify Your name in our lives.

I surrender our future into Your loving hands, trusting that You know what's best for us. May Your will be done in our lives, and may our relationship be centered on You, with my future husband leading our household with humility, faith, and a servant's heart.

IN JESUS' NAME, I PRAY,
AMEN."

Prayer for Gratitude and Humility

"Dear Divine Creator,

I come to you with a heart full of gratitude for the gift of love and companionship that you have planned for my life. I am thankful for the future husband you have chosen for me, a man who will be a blessing and a partner in this journey of life.

I ask for the grace of humility, to recognize the beauty and uniqueness of the person you have destined for me. Grant me the wisdom to appreciate and cherish the qualities that make him who he is, embracing both his strengths and weaknesses.

May I approach this union with a humble heart, acknowledging that love is a gift from You and that a healthy and loving relationship requires understanding, patience, and empathy. Help me to be a supportive partner, nurturing a relationship built on trust, respect, and kindness. Guide me to be grateful every day for the presence of my future husband in my life. May I express my gratitude through words and actions, showing him love, compassion, and encouragement.

As I wait for this beautiful union to unfold, I trust in Your divine timing and plan for my life. May I remain open-hearted and prepared to receive the love that you have destined for me.

Thank you for the blessings of love and companionship that you bring into my life. I surrender my hopes, dreams, and desires for my future husband into Your loving hands.

AMEN."

JOURNEY TOGETHER

In anticipation of and preparation for your journey together, this section includes prayers devoted to your relationship with your future husband. Blessings are requested for the connection you will have, your dialogue, your trust, and the love and dedication that will serve as the cornerstone of your partnership.

You travel a route full of hope, faith, and expectation toward a shared life with your future husband. In order to ask God for direction, favors, and the development of a solid, God-centered relationship, these prayers have been carefully considered.

Prayer for me about my Preparation for my future husband

"Heavenly Father,

I come before you with a heart filled with gratitude for the love and guidance you continuously bestow upon me. As I walk on this journey of life, I lift up my aspirations and desires for my future husband to you.

Grant me the wisdom to prepare myself in mind, body, and spirit for the union with the man you have destined for me. Help me cultivate virtues of kindness, patience, understanding, and unconditional love within myself. May I grow in selflessness and compassion, ready to embrace the responsibilities and joys of a committed relationship. Guide my steps as I strive to become the best version of myself. Help me to develop a strong and faithful heart, one that is capable of nurturing a loving and enduring partnership. Grant me the grace to cultivate virtues that will make me a supportive, respectful, and loving partner.

Lord, I ask for your discernment in recognizing and embracing the person you have chosen for me. May our paths cross at the perfect time according to your divine plan. Help me to trust in your timing and remain patient, knowing that you have a purpose for everything.

May my love for you, Lord, be the cornerstone of my preparation, seeking your guidance in every step I take towards this future blessed union. Let my actions and intentions be guided by your love and grace.

In your infinite wisdom, prepare both my heart and the heart of my future husband, that when the time is right, our union may reflect your divine love and bring glory to your name.

I entrust my hopes, dreams, and preparations into your loving hands, dear Lord. May your will be done in my life.

IN JESUS' NAME, I PRAY. AMEN."

May this prayer bring you peace and strength as you continue your journey in preparation for your future husband. Trust in the divine plan and continue to seek guidance from above in all your endeavors.

Prayer for me about Understanding Communication

"Heavenly Father,

I come before you with a heart full of gratitude for the gift of love and the prospect of a future with my beloved. As I journey towards the path of union with my future husband, I ask for your guidance and blessing, particularly in the aspect of communication.

Grant me the wisdom to express my thoughts, feelings, and desires openly and honestly. Help me to listen attentively, to understand without judgment, and to communicate with patience, kindness, and empathy.

May our conversations be filled with respect, trust, and genuine understanding. Strengthen our bond through effective and compassionate communication, enabling us to grow closer to each other and to You.

Lord, I pray for the grace to navigate challenges that may arise in our communication, to find peaceful resolutions, and to always approach one another with love and grace. I trust in Your divine plan and timing for our relationship. Help us to build a strong foundation based on mutual respect and effective communication, laying the groundwork for a blessed and harmonious future together. In Your loving hands, I place my intentions and aspirations for this aspect of my relationship. Guide me, dear Lord, as I prepare to share my life and heart with my future husband.

IN JESUS' NAME, I PRAY,
AMEN."

prayer for me about Trust and Commitment for my future husband

"Heavenly Father,

As I journey through life, I bring before you my hopes and dreams, especially those regarding my future husband. I pray for the gift of trust and unwavering faith in Your divine plan for both of us.

Grant me the strength to cultivate a deep sense of trust in Your timing and guidance, knowing that You hold our futures in Your loving hands. Help me to surrender my worries and fears, placing my trust in Your perfect will for my life and for the life of my future husband.

May I develop the patience to wait for the right person, to trust that You are preparing us both for a fulfilling and loving union built on commitment and faithfulness.

Lord, instill within me a heart that understands the true essence of commitment—a commitment not only to each other but also to You. May our relationship be grounded in mutual respect, honesty, and unwavering dedication, reflecting the commitment we have made to honor and cherish one another.

Guide my future husband as well, preparing his heart and mind for the journey ahead. Help us both to grow individually so that we may complement and support each other in our shared path.

Grant me wisdom to recognize and embrace the qualities of trustworthiness and commitment in my future partner. Help us to build a relationship founded on love, respect, and devotion to You and each other.

I surrender our future into Your hands, trusting that You will lead us together in Your perfect timing. May our relationship be a testament to Your grace and faithfulness.

IN YOUR NAME, I PRAY,

AMEN."

My Prayer for Love and Forgiveness

"Dear Divine Creator,

I come before you today with a heart filled with gratitude and hope. As I journey toward a future with my beloved, I ask for your guidance and blessings.

Grant me the strength to love unconditionally, to embrace my future husband with an open heart, and to cherish the bond we will share. Help me understand that love is not merely a feeling but a conscious choice to nurture, support, and uplift each other through life's highs and lows.

I pray for the gift of forgiveness, understanding that none of us are perfect. May I be quick to forgive and slow to hold onto grievances, knowing that forgiveness is an essential part of a healthy and enduring relationship. Help me release any past hurts and allow space in my heart for compassion and understanding.

May our relationship be built on a foundation of mutual respect, trust, and kindness. Guide us to communicate openly and honestly, fostering an environment where our love can grow and flourish.

I pray for my future husband as well. May he be surrounded by your grace, filled with love, and guided by wisdom and understanding. Grant him the strength to face challenges and the humility to seek forgiveness when needed.

Together, may we create a life filled with joy, support, and unwavering love. May our love story be a testament to your grace and the power of love and forgiveness.

IN YOUR NAME, I PRAY. AMEN."

Prayer To God For his Guidance To Pick Right Partner

Dear God,

I come before you seeking your guidance and wisdom as I navigate the path of finding a life partner. You know the desires of my heart and the qualities I seek in a companion. Help me discern with clarity and understanding as I make this important decision.

Grant me the patience to wait for the right person and the strength to recognize them when they come into my life. Open my eyes to see beyond superficial qualities and guide me towards someone who shares my values, aspirations, and faith.

May your divine light shine upon my path, illuminating the way towards a relationship built on love, trust, and mutual respect. Help me to understand that your timing is perfect, and that waiting for the right person is worth it.

Give me the wisdom to recognize red flags and the courage to walk away from relationships that are not aligned with your will for my life. Let your peace fill my heart as I seek a partner who will support and encourage me in my journey with you.

Above all, Lord, let your will be done in this aspect of my life. Lead me to the person you have chosen for me, someone with whom I can grow spiritually, emotionally, and mentally.

I surrender my desires and intentions to you, trusting that you have a beautiful plan for my life. Guide me, dear God, as I seek to find the one whom you have intended for me. In your holy name, I pray.

AMEN.

Prayer for Our Blessed Union

"Divine and Merciful Creator,

I come to you with a heart filled with hope and faith, seeking your guidance and blessings as I journey towards union with my future husband. I trust in your divine plan and timing, knowing that you have prepared someone special for me, a partner to share life's joys and challenges. I pray for my future husband, wherever he may be, that you watch over him, protect him, and guide him towards our destined meeting. May you fill his heart with kindness, love, and understanding. Grant him strength, wisdom, and courage as he walks his path.

Lord, as I prepare myself for this blessed union, help me cultivate qualities of patience, compassion, and grace. Grant me the wisdom to recognize and cherish the love that blossoms between us, and the strength to nurture it through every season of life.

I pray for a relationship built on mutual respect, trust, and unwavering commitment. May our love be a reflection of your unconditional love, resilient in times of joy and adversity.

Bless our future union, dear Father. May it be a source of joy, support, and growth for both of us.

May we find happiness in each other's arms and be united in our faith and devotion to you.
I surrender my hopes and desires for this future union into your loving hands, trusting that you know what is best for me. Grant me the patience to wait for the right time and the discernment to recognize the one you have chosen for me. In your divine grace, I place my trust and my heart's desires.

AMEN."

May this prayer bring you comfort and strength as you await the beautiful union destined for you.

CONCLUSION

As you reach the end of this collection of prayers dedicated to your future husband, I hope that these words have served as a source of inspiration, comfort, and guidance in your journey of anticipation and preparation.

The act of prayer is a powerful and intimate connection with the divine—a channel through which we express our hopes, dreams, and desires. In dedicating these prayers to your future husband, you have laid a beautiful foundation of love, faith, and support for the man who will eventually walk alongside you in life.

Remember, these prayers are not merely words on a page but expressions of your deepest intentions, hopes, and aspirations. Each prayer is a testament to your love, care, and commitment to nurturing a relationship grounded in faith, love, and mutual respect.

As you continue on this journey, I encourage you to hold onto the essence of these prayers—seeking God's guidance, blessings, and grace for your future husband in every season of life. Embrace the wisdom found in these words, adapt them to your own heart's desires, and let them serve as a reminder of the love and dedication you hold for your future partner.

May these prayers accompany you as you eagerly anticipate the moment when your paths will intertwine, and may they continue to resonate in your heart as you nurture a relationship that honors God and glorifies His name.

Thanks for your purchase, hope you enjoyed reading. Could you please take a few seconds to leave a positive feedback on this book?

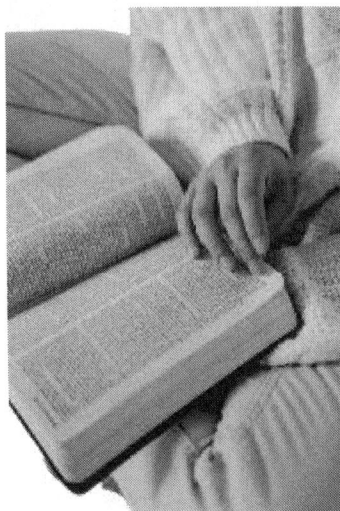

BONUS

PRAYER Journal `date:` [_____]

Note To Self

PRAYER Journal

Note To Self

PRAYER Journal

date: _____

Note To Self

PRAYER Journal

date: _____

Note To Self

PRAYER Journal

date: _____

Note To Self

PRAYER Journal

date: _____

Note To Self

PRAYER Journal

date:

Note To Self

PRAYER Journal

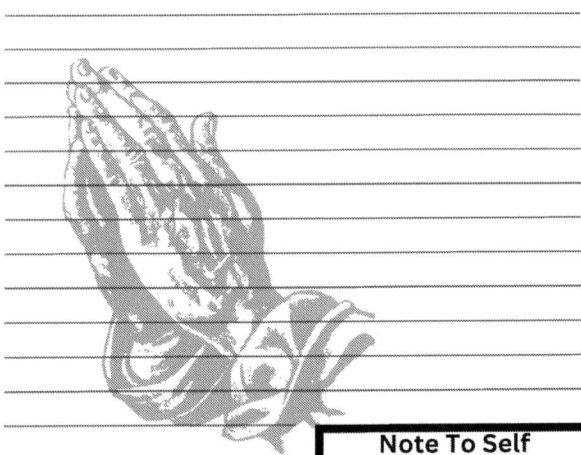

date: _____

Note To Self

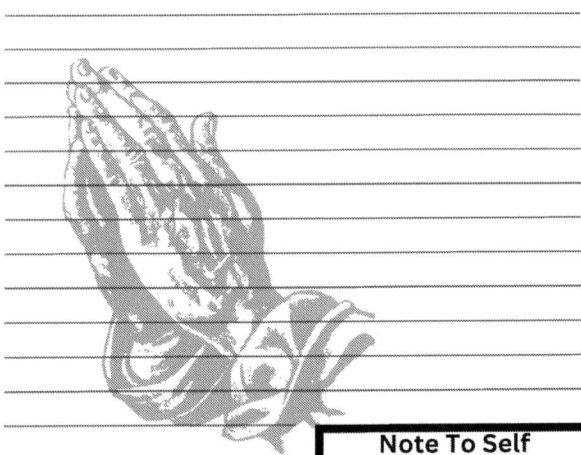

PRAYER Journal

date: _____

Note To Self

PRAYER Journal

date: _____

Note To Self

PRAYER Journal

date: _____

Note To Self

PRAYER Journal

date: _____

Note To Self

PRAYER Journal

date: _____

Note To Self

PRAYER Journal

Note To Self

PRAYER Journal

date: _____

Note To Self

PRAYER Journal

date: _____

Note To Self

PRAYER Journal

Note To Self

PRAYER Journal

date: _____

Note To Self

PRAYER Journal

Note To Self

PRAYER Journal

date: _____

_____
_____
_____
_____
_____
_____
_____
_____
_____
_____
_____
_____
_____

Note To Self

_____
_____
_____
_____
_____

Made in the USA
Middletown, DE
07 January 2024

47378711R00050